For You, *My Friend*

For You, *My Friend*

An Insightful Guide for Thoughtful Skeptics

by

Scott Morton

Dawson**Media**

ISBN 978-1-935-65136-9

Unless otherwise identified, all Scripture quotations in this publication are taken from the HOLY BIBLE, NEW INTERNATIONAL VERSION® (NIV®). Copyright © 1973, 1978, 1984, 2011 by Biblica Inc. Used by permission.

Printed in the United States of America.
18 17 16 15 14 13   2 3 4 5 6 7 8 9

Dedicated to my skeptical friend,
and other fellow skeptics wherever you may be.

Preface

Where do you turn for spiritual direction when you're skeptical of old churches, new churches, mega-churches, TV preachers with poofy hair, and new-age philosophies championed by drug-rehabbed celebrities? Deep down, you suspect Somebody's out there who truly cares about you, but you don't want to become religious or weird. Advice from your friends, though sincere, is full of its own painful baggage. And you are not helped by the Marilyn Monroe quip, "I believe in everything—a little bit."

This little booklet cuts through religiosity to give you twelve solid markers on which to evaluate your spiritual instincts. You might call them universal laws about life, happiness, and eternity that resonate deep inside—no matter what your background.

I admit I bring a bias to this topic (we all do). I too am a skeptic about easy answers and black-and-white opinions that drain the Supernatural of mystery. I don't have it all figured out. And yes, I am still a class "A" sinner! But I have had experiences with God that defy explanation. All the religious leaders I study have something to contribute, but I am more attracted to Jesus of Nazareth than any other. He is different and He has affected me deeply.

I commend you for expressing doubts and asking hard questions. Author Tim Keller says, "A faith without doubts is like a body without any antibodies in it."[1] Whether you are churched, un-churched, or de-churched, as you read this booklet I hope you bring an honest longing to experience a meaningful spiritual journey. And bring humility too. You've seen in others what arrogance produces. Enjoy the trip.

[1] *The Reason for God,* Tim Keller; Riverhead Books, New York, 2009, page xvii.

1. Life is not fair.

This is the theological version of the bumper sticker: "S— Happens." The careful driver sideswipes a guardrail. The health food expert dies of a heart attack. The loyal worker loses a promotion to the CEO's nephew. Life's not fair, so we hire lawyers to assuage our pain and suffering. As long as we can take someone to court, we can cope with disappointment. But sometimes, there's no one to sue.

At a dinner party a friend told me he had cancer. "Throat cancer," he said. "I almost died." As I expressed my concern, he waved me off. "Too much smoking," he interrupted. He was not bitter. Perhaps because his personal tragedy was caused by his own actions. But what about those with throat cancer who have never smoked? What about those who are paralyzed because they happened to be in the path of a drunk driver? Those are big unfairnesses.

What about little unfairnesses? Your opportunistic supervisor takes credit for your web design. A careless waiter spills ranch dressing on your new purple blouse. Your son's buddy parks his oil-dripping '67 Mustang on your immaculate concrete driveway "just for a minute." If allowed to fester, even small unfairnesses can produce bitter, angry people.

With unfairness we often look for someone or something to blame—sometimes a person, sometimes an industry, sometimes God. To thrive, bitterness must have an object to hate. People who choose bitterness as their way to handle unfairness make themselves miserable, and they make others miserable.

Instead of bitterness, some people choose its sophisticated cousin—resentment. Resentment-people submerge their pain, but it escapes through alcohol, anger, workaholism, or self-loathing. Though not as obvious as bitterness, resentment kills joy and inhibits love.

Are we doomed? No. I've discovered that resentment always begins with a disappointment. When I specifically identify my disappointments, I no longer need to live out of my woundedness and become hard-wired to wound others. Those who don't deal with their pain pass it on.

Can you think of unfairnesses in your life? Little ones, like your brother not paying his share for your parents' Christmas gift. Or childhood friends' merciless teasing about your bird-skinny legs. Or big ones, like a spouse who cheated.

Where would your personal unfairnesses appear on this timeline?

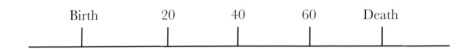

It is not the unfairnesses and difficulties in life that determine what kind of person we become, but rather how we respond.

How are you responding?

> "One ship sails east and another west
> By the selfsame winds that blow,
> 'Tis the set of the sails
> And not the gales,
> That tells the way we go.

"Like the waves of the sea are the waves of time,
As we journey along through life,
'Tis the set of the soul
That determines the goal,
And not the calm or the strife."

—Ella Wheeler Wilcox
(American Writer 1850-1919)

2. If you focus on being happy, you won't be.

When you ask people about their life dreams today, many say they "just want to be happy." Or they want their kids to be happy. Fair enough. But how? More leisure time? More adult toys? Spending more time together as a family? Can we be happier by trying to be happier? In the 1980's Bobby McFerrin sang, "Don't worry. Be happy!" It's simple.

In the Bible, the word translated "happy" appears only 26 times. For something so important, you'd think it would be a major Bible theme. Similarly, philosophers say more about where happiness is not found than where to find it. "If we want to know what happiness is we must seek it, not as if it were a pot of gold at the end of a rainbow. . . ." [1]

You've already discovered that lasting happiness is not found in accumulating material stuff. Haven't you? Or in having power? Or great sex? Similarly, spending money on ourselves or our family, playing tons of golf, eating at nice restaurants exhilarates us, but our happiness meter doesn't match our expectations and usually leaves us feeling more empty than before we started. Though they make grand promises, possessions, power, and pleasure make us happy only for a season. Simply put, happiness is a byproduct. It pops up when you aim at something else. People seem happiest when they are giving, serving, helping others. "There is in happiness an element of self-forgetfulness. You lose yourself in something outside yourself when you are happy; just as when you are desperately miserable you are intensely conscious of yourself, [you] are a solid little lump of ego weighing a ton." [2]

Stop focusing on me—my "solid little lump of ego"? In today's world, not focusing on self is counter-cultural, even risky. But Bob Dylan's latest CD disagrees with Bobbie McFerrin. Dylan sings, "Gonna forget about myself for awhile, gonna see what others need." Hmmm.

[1] W. Beran Wolfe, *Light from Many Lamps,* edited by Lillian Eichler Watson, Simon and Schuster, New York, 1951, page 12.
[2] J.B. Priestly, ibid, page 14.

3. Everybody dies.

No surprise here. Or as Woody Allen puts it, "I know I'm going to die; I just don't want to be there when it happens." Despite the finality of death, people are witty about it.

> "The last thing that I've been unable to control in my quest
> to control everything around me is death."[1]
> —Lars Ulrich, Metallica drummer

> "How do you know when you're old? When you double your age
> and realize you're not going to live that long."[2]
> —Michael J. Leyden III

Americans even know "how" they'll die. Here are the top ten causes of death in America according to the Centers for Disease Control and Prevention in Atlanta:

1. Heart Disease
2. Cancer
3. Stroke
4. Lung Disease
5. Accidents
6. Pneumonia-Influenza
7. Diabetes
8. HIV-AIDS
9. Suicide
10. Liver Disease-Cirrhosis

Eight of these can be modified if we eat less fatty food, smoke fewer cigarettes, and worry less. By altering our personal behavior, we "reduce our risk of dying early by 70-80 percent."[3] But our chance of dying is still 100 percent. Millions are spent each year to slow the aging process. Thanks to Elizabeth Arden and Bally's Health Clubs, some of us are extremely well preserved.

For You, *My Friend*

Even if we admit we will die, we don't know when, as illustrated by a postcard addressed to James Day in Wales.[4] The back of the card said:

> Dear Friend,
> Just a line to show that I am alive and kicking and going grand. It's a treat.
> > Yours,
> > WJR

The front of the postcard showed the new four-funneled steamer, the *Titanic*. WJR was one of the 1,500 who went down with that great ship. Not only will you and I die, we may, like WJR, die before we intend to, while we're still "kicking and going grand."

The life expectancy of an American born in 1900 was 47.3 years. Today it is 75. If you transfer these 75 years to a 24-hour clock and you are now 25, it's 8:00 a.m. If you are 38, it's 12:00 noon—your life is half over. If you're 50, you've learned much that could help others, but it's 4:00 p.m. Twilight is coming. At age 55 it's 5:35 p.m. At 60 it's 7:10 p.m. At 70 it's 10:20 p.m. Every birthday means another 19 minutes has elapsed. Gather ye rosebuds while ye may.

As President William McKinley lay dying of an assassin's bullet in 1900, his wife sobbed by his bedside, "I want to go, too," she said. Weakly, McKinley replied, "You will, my dear, you will."[5]

"Why, you do not even know what will happen tomorrow. What is your life? You are a mist that appears for a little while and then vanishes."
—James 4:14

"Remind yourself daily that you are going to die."[6]
—*The Rule of St. Benedict 4:47*

[1] Quoted in *Newsweek*, June 9, 2003 (from *Christianity Today* Sept-Oct 2003).

[2] As quoted in *Forbes*, November 25, 1991.

[3] *Parade Magazine*, March 10, 1996, page 19.

[4] Michael Ryan, *Parade Magazine*, June 15,1997.

[5] *Book of Last Words*. As quoted in *The New Yorker Magazine*.

[6] *Christianity Today*, December, 2008, page 55.

4. There are no U-Hauls at funerals.

In other words, you can't take it with you. After you die, all your stuff stays here, including the customized home you built with 29 subcontractors, your vintage Corvette, your Sears table saw, your antique cups and saucers, your Bowflex, your iPhone, even your American Express card—you *will* leave home without it! Everything you worked hard to get is now placed into the hands of your heirs and their attorneys—if you made a will. If you didn't make a will, then it's simply placed in the hands of attorneys.

Even though I know I can't take it with me, I sometimes forget. When I'm too "frugal," my wife asks, "Would you like me to tuck $20 bills around you in your coffin?" Actually, frugal is my word. "Tight" is hers.

"Surely everyone goes around like a mere phantom; in vain they rush about, heaping up wealth without knowing whose it will finally be."
—Psalm 39:6

Do you have friends or family who think that the next thing they purchase will bring fulfillment? Or more fulfillment? What is behind this passion for accumulating things? Will a new electronic gadget or the latest facial cream dissolve the feeling that they are a tiny, nameless tadpole swimming in an uncaring ocean of material-ism? Shopping is not lasting therapy!

Jesus of Nazareth said it this way: "Watch out! Be on your guard against all kinds of greed; a man's life does not consist in the abundance of his possessions" (Luke 12:15). He who dies with the most toys may win—but he leaves them all here.

5. Death is not the end.

What happens five seconds after you die? Carl Sagan, science writer and Cornell University astronomer says: nothing! "I would love to believe that when I die I will live again, that some thinking, feeling, remembering part of me will continue. But as much as I want to believe that, and despite the ancient and worldwide cultural traditions that assert an afterlife, I know of nothing to suggest it is more than wishful thinking."[1]

Sagan's belief is called nihilism—we are physical beings only. Within homo sapiens an eternal soul does not exist. Heaven and hell are foolishness. The "thinking, feeling, remembering" part of us dies with our bodies. Like tomato plants, we grow, bloom, bear fruit, and return to the ground. It's over.

Famous physicist, Stephen Hawking agrees. "The human brain is like a computer that will stop working when it's components fail. There is no heaven or afterlife for broken-down computers; that is a fairy story for people afraid of the dark."[2]

Instinctively, something cries out within each of us that we are more than tomato plants, but who will disagree with Carl Sagan and Stephen Hawking? "If we do indeed possess an immaterial soul," physicist Victor Stenger writes in God: *The Failed Hypothesis,* "then we should expect to find some evidence for it."[3] Can we?

Does the fact that every culture on earth has (or had) a belief system regarding the eternal existence of the soul prove the afterlife? Egyptians placed food in pharaohs' tombs; ancient South American tribes sacrificed young men and women to accompany the departed.

Though universal assertion of an afterlife doesn't make it so, it does show a universal longing for life after death, which, according to Sagan, is nothing more than "wishful thinking" or a "fairy story for people afraid of the dark." But where did that longing come from? Do animals have it?

What about those who have come back to life from clinical death? Many can vividly describe their out-of-body and back-from-death experiences and often see a bright light. Or are they reacting to their body shutting down?

In the book, *Heaven is for Real,* a three-year-old described what he saw in heaven during his near-death experience in the hospital—details about his family members who had already died that he couldn't have possibly known about. Death experiences may not conclusively prove we have a soul, but they must not be ignored.

Proving an afterlife falls short scientifically, but nihilism falls short scientifically too. It's a step of faith to trust there is life after death, but it's also a step of faith to trust there is only death after death! If there is nothing after death, at least one of the following assumptions must be accepted by faith:

1. Man is not an eternal being. You and I have no soul—no "thinking, feeling, remembering" part. The impulse crying out inside us for something beyond death is wishful thinking.
2. If (while physically alive) we have a soul, it ceases to exist at death. If there is a higher power, it cannot (or chooses not) to keep our soul functioning.
3. Every culture of the world is wrong to believe in an afterlife.

The nihilist who marginalizes those who believe in an afterlife walks on thin ice himself.

Is there a more reasonable view? University of Southern California philosopher

Dallas Willard repositions the question from faith to reasonableness: "Is it truly reasonable to think that we will continue beyond the demise of our bodies?"[4] He says yes.

The fact that we are conscious and can talk to ourselves about ourselves points to something within us that is more than mere physical matter. And what about the ability to make moral choices which seems unique to homo sapiens? There's something inside us besides "survival of the fittest" instincts. How and when did man become so different from other animals? Physical death is not the end if a powerful God truly exists outside our own imagination.

> "…A God of infinite love would not create finite persons and then drop them out of existence when the potentialities of their nature, including their awareness of himself, have only just begun to be realized."[5]
> —John Hicks

The Apostle Paul understood it this way: "For we know that if the earthly tent we live in is destroyed, we have a building from God, an eternal house in heaven, not built by human hands" (2 Corinthians 5:1).

Poets often see scientific truths before scientists. Look carefully at Longfellow's last two lines:

> Tell me not in mournful numbers,
> Life is but an empty dream!—
> For the soul is dead that slumbers,
> And things are not what they seem.
> Life is real! Life is earnest!
> And the grave is not the goal;
> Dust thou art, to dust returneth
> Was not spoken of the soul.[6]

If you and I are merely accidents of random biological processes, there is no afterlife. But assuming we are alone in the universe with all the other tomato plants is a leap of faith! Death is not the end. But only if we are designed by a non-imaginary transcendent power.

[1] Carl Sagan, *Parade Magazine,* March 10, 1996, page 19.

[2] As quoted in the *Colorado Springs Gazette,* May 17, 2011.

[3] Dinesh D'Souza, *What's So Great About Christianity?* Tyndale, Carol Stream, IL, 2007, page 244.

[4] Dallas Willard, *The Divine Conspiracy,* San Francisco: Harper, 1998, page 388.

[5] John Hick, *The Center of Christianity* (San Francisco: Harper and Row, 1978), page 106.

[6] "A Psalm of Life," Henry Wadsworth Longfellow, *Light From Many Lamps,* Simon and Shuster, New York, 1979, page 125

6. He is there and He is not silent.

Atheists argue that God can't scientifically be "there." And they imply that believers are gullible, non-scientific simpletons. Late-night talk show host Bill Maher produced a documentary debunking religion, *Religulous.* He exposed some religious practices as dumb—he's right. Some religious practices are dumb. But Maher didn't say there is no God: he said it is impossible to know for sure. Carl Sagan goes further with his famous quote: "The cosmos is all there is, or was, or ever will be."

By contrast, since 1944 Gallup.com polls repeatedly show that 92-98 percent of Americans "believe in God." Can we conclude that since the majority believe in God, he or she or it must be there? The majority also believed the earth was flat, that space travel was impossible, that home-computers would never be popular, and that actors could never become governors of California.

Majority rule does not prove God exists. What the 92-98 percent does prove is that people want to believe in a higher power. Is it possible that even if there were no God we would invent one because we need one so badly? Perhaps columnist Don

Feder is right when he said, "It seems as though a hunger for the Creator is imprinted on the human heart."[1]

But is the higher power an imaginary "something" I create in my mind? That's all some people think religion is—giving obeisance to a made-up god. If that's the case, then Maher is right—it is dumb! Well-meaning perhaps. But still dumb.

Recently, on a popular talk radio program, the host was receiving calls about a tragic auto accident that claimed the life of a young mother and her small child. Some callers said that though we can't understand it, we must assume it is God's will. The next caller lamented the kind of God who would permit a young mother to die. Then he said stunningly: "'My God' wouldn't do that."

Though sounding noble, this caller's god is built from the ground up based on his version of right and wrong—a reflection of his own values. Of course, we don't want God to take human life capriciously, but we must be careful of creating a "god" in our own image when we don't understand why bad things happen.

When pressed, most of us want to believe there is Someone outside ourselves who is greater than ourselves—"transcendent" is the theological word. No one said it better than former Russian Premier Nikita Khrushchev on a visit to America in the

1950's: "I do not believe in God, and God knows I don't believe in Him."
Is it possible to prove the existence of a personal God? For centuries, thick books have been written on "The Question of God." I've dabbled in a few; here are three clues for the existence of a higher power:

1. The Uncaused First-Cause Argument

Science asserts that everything in existence has a cause, including the universe. The universe could not have invented itself.

> "Almost everyone now believes that the universe, and time itself,
> had a beginning at the Big Bang."[2]
> —Stephen Hawking, physicist

A simple clue: scientists have proven that the universe has been expanding for millions of years; therefore, it must have previously been contained in a much smaller area. The expanding universe behaves like heat escaping from a kitchen stove. Heat expands through the room from that "explosion" of opening the oven door.

Perhaps we should call God "First Cause." In my Iowa high school for the spring concert our chorus sang the classic piece, "The heavens are telling the glory of God." I didn't understand it then, but I do now. The heavens point to the existence of an Uncaused First-Cause.

The idea that the universe has always existed, that it was caused by nothing, has now lost favor with scientists as being unscientific.

2. The Design Argument

Scientists agree that the universe displays amazing order. Again Hawking: "It would be very difficult to explain why the universe would have begun just this way except as an act of a god who intended to create beings like us."[3]

Perhaps you've heard the clockmaker story. Imagine traveling across a vast treeless plain, hour after hour. No civilization. No animals. No vegetation. No Sirius radio. Suddenly you stumble over a small alarm clock at your feet. You immediately glance around, scanning the horizon. Nothing.

Despite the lack of life, you conclude that the clock could not have arrived because of random forces. There must be a "clockmaker" somewhere—a master designer.

3. The Moral Argument

If there is no higher power, then we are amoral animals—our highest instinct is survival. Although some higher animals possess altruistic tendencies, they are not primarily guided by moral obligations as they eat, mate, or kill.

> **"How is it that inanimate matter can organize itself to contemplate itself?"[4]**
> **—Allan Sandage, cosmologist**

Furthermore, scientists warn us about anthropomorphism—introducing human emotions into animal behavior. You see it on nature channels with non-scientific narration like this: "The mother gazelle knows the dry season is coming soon and that she must find water for her babies." Really. How do we know she thinks that? Perhaps you've seen the popular film clip of adult water buffaloes coming to the aid of a buffalo calf who was snapped up in the jaws of a crocodile at an African watering hole. In a frenzy, adult buffaloes attacked the crocodile so aggressively that the calf escaped. I asked a professor of evolution about that incident and he surprised me by saying, "Yes, the adult buffaloes acted to save the calf, but they would not have given their lives in the process."

That is one way homo sapiens is different! Throughout history, brave men and woman have died willingly to save others, not out of instinct, but by their own moral decisions. That's huge! If we are merely amoral highly developed animals, at what point in our evolution did we gain this "conscience?"

Furthermore, all cultures, past or present, have moral codes. These moral codes, such as protecting the weak or pledging loyalty to family, are often similar across diverse cultures, protecting the innocent for example. That these codes universally exist points to a transcendent God behind them. Apologist and writer C.S. Lewis called this the "law of decent behavior."

Finally, here's an unconvincing argument from your friends. "God helped me, there-ore He exists." Many religious people cannot explain the existence of God except through personal stories where God answered a prayer, cured an illness, or saved a job. Please be patient with them. Although their warm personal testimonies may not convince you, they might contain clues for a transcendent God. Don't negate God's existence merely because your friends are not articulate. Intellectual arguments for believing can be found.

But let's flip the question: Can we prove that a higher power does *not exist*? How would we set up a cosmic experiment to show convincingly nothing is there? How big a test tube would we need!

Science fiction author, Isaac Asimov, concludes: "Emotionally I am an atheist. I don't have the evidence to prove that God doesn't exist, but I so strongly suspect that he doesn't that I don't want to waste my time."5 Let's face it, arguments for or against God's existence do not ultimately persuade us. If Isaac Asimov cannot dismiss the "Uncaused First Cause," then you and I must not either.

Philosopher and author, Francis Schaeffer, said it this way, "He is there and he is not silent." Either a transcendent creator-designer exists or it doesn't. The only way to know for sure is to experience the Designer personally. Is that possible?

For You, *My Friend*

[1] Don Feder, *USA Today*, April 16, 2007, page 11a.

[2] *The Reason For God,* Timothy Keller, Riverhead Books, New York, 2008, Page 133.

[3] Ibid. Page 134.

[4] *The Case For Faith,* Lee Stroebel, Zondervan, Grand Rapids, 2000, page 92.

[5] From "Isaac Asimov on Science and the Bible," interview with Paul Kurtz, published in *Free Inquiry,* Spring 1982, www.sullivan-county.com/id3/asimov2.htm.

7. Having faith doesn't mean kissing your brains goodbye.

Is faith opposed to facts, science, and common sense? Have you heard about the little boy whose teacher asked him to define faith? He said, "Faith is believing something you know ain't true."

Some people say that faith is all you need. They say that faith changed their lives, but sometimes they have closed their minds to science and common sense. If faith in God is legitimate, must we ignore our intellect? No, faith and science are not mutually exclusive.

To understand faith we must first ask, "Faith in what?" For example, a TV reporter asks a fireman who heroically fought a fire, "What kept you from quitting?" The hero says, "Faith! Faith kept me going even though I wanted to quit."

But faith in what?

Faith must have an object. For example, this morning as I drive to work I will exert faith that the drivers in the oncoming lanes will stay in their lanes. I also have faith that the BMW guy racing in from the right will stop at the stoplight. I proceed through the intersection by "faith" assuming he will stop.

What is my faith in? I am trusting that other drivers—complete strangers—will obey the traffic laws. That is not always wise, but my point is that faith must have an object.

Another example. The chair I am sitting in today is sturdy, but it is 20 years old. The upholstery is worn and a spring pops out of the bottom now and then, but it holds me up. Question: Am I held up because I have faith in the chair or because of the chair itself?

Many pseudo-religious people would answer that my faith in the chair holds me up. But even without faith the chair holds me up. The schoolboy's definition of faith is dead wrong. Instead how about this?

Faith is trusting that which you have good reasons to suspect is true.

Personal question: What is the object of your faith? What are you trusting in? It cannot be faith in faith. Once you have identified the object then you must ask if that object is trustworthy? Is it worthy of your faith?

8. Drawing close to God starts with gratitude.

Thanksgiving morning I arose early to a cold, gray overcast sky. In the east a reddish-orange glow peeped under the horizon, bouncing off low-hanging gray clouds. It intensified and lessened every few seconds. In less than a minute, it was gone. Nice.

And then (as many Americans do) I sat down to my Thanksgiving Day custom of listing "Ten Things for which I Am Thankful." Glancing out the window, I listed first the beautiful orange-gray sky. Then it occurred to me: The beauty of the sky this morning was a gift to everyone in our city—rich or poor, homeless or home-owner, happy or sad, Republican or Democrat, gay or straight. It didn't matter if our citizens believed in a Creator. Even those who hated God could enjoy beauty that Thanksgiving morning.

The words of Jesus of Nazareth came to mind: "He causes his sun to rise on the evil and the good, and sends rain on the righteous and the unrighteous" (Matthew 5:45).

God gives a gorgeous sunrise to all His creatures, whether they acknowledge Him or not. If I were God, pretty sunrises and life-giving rains would come only to those who appreciate me or give money to erase the carbon footprint or to save the endangered Preble's Jumping Mouse. I would definitely not give rains to those who throw litter from car windows!

But (unlike me) God gives gracious gifts to all—even litter people! Our response? Thank you. The great theologian from 500 years ago, Martin Luther, said that even though people "are completely surrounded by his gifts they have gotten used to them. . . . They say, 'What's so special about the fact that the sun shines, fire gives warmth, the ocean provides fish, the earth yields grain, cows have calves . . . and hens lay eggs? These things happen every day! Is something insignificant because it happens every day?"[1]

Before we can experience God, we must acknowledge what we already possess. Here are three things everyone can be thankful for:

1. **The gift of nature**—a beautiful sunrise, bumblebees that defy gravity, Alaskan beetles that survive sub-zero temperatures because they have some sort of anti-freeze. Wow.

2. **The gift of time**—you didn't die in the night. My Uncle Garvin used to say, "Every new day is a gift."

> "You wake up in the morning, and lo! Your purse is magically filled with
> 24 hours of the unmanufactured tissue of the universe of your life.
> It is yours! It is the most precious of possessions."[2]
> —Arnold Bennett

3. **The gift of a consistent universe**—what if gravity worked only on Tuesdays? What if the speed of light slowed down or sped up erratically? What if water boiled at a different temperature each week?

The laws of physics are consistent, not capricious. Where did that consistency come from? One problem with atheism is the question: To whom does an atheist say "thank you"?

Some add to their Top Ten lists things like friends, family, employment, an iPhone. Okay, but not everyone has all that. But everyone can enjoy a sunrise.

Is thanking God absolutely necessary? Doesn't He know I'm grateful? Why do I need to verbalize it? Maybe it's more for me than God. When I genuinely say thank you to my wife, a business associate, or the hassled minimum-wage single mom clerk at the fast food restaurant, something inside me relaxes. It helps me become less narcissistic. It pushes me toward thinking about others.

Without a proactive, thankful spirit I am headed toward self-centeredness, which easily leads to bitterness and resentment—especially when tough times come my way. Being thankful is an antidote to bitterness.

But there's a second reason to be thankful: A grateful spirit is crucial to avoid faulty thinking about God. The early Christian leader, Paul the Apostle, warned:

"For although they knew God, they neither glorified him as God nor gave thanks to him, but their thinking became futile and their foolish hearts were darkened. Although they claimed to be wise, they became fools and exchanged the glory of the immortal God for images made to look like a mortal human being. . . ."
—Romans 1:21-23

Paul says the downward spiral of worshipping something of our own invention starts by not honoring God "as God." By contrast, a thankful spirit acknowledges what is! Without gratefulness, I speculate about a "god" I would prefer. And when I speculate about what "my god" is like, "my god" becomes a lot like me. It all ends in foolishness.

The writer of the Old Testament Psalms quotes what God said to Israel as they made lame excuses for thieves to go free and to speak deceit to one another: "You thought I [God] was exactly like you," (Psalms 50:21).

Through history people of all cultures have tended to re-make God in their own image—from the ground up. And it starts with thanklessness and failing to honor God as God. But thankfulness recognizes God as what He truly is.

When I was a kid, I remember lassoing fence posts in our farm yard with my clothes-line cowboy lariat. In a pensive moment I thought, "What if I was a fence post? No fun with friends. No birthday presents. No baseball. No breathing." At that moment I remember thanking God that I was alive and not a fence post.

That's why six-year-olds don't write theology books! But even though I hadn't heard of Romans 1, my momentary ounce of thankfulness was the right response to a loving Creator who brought about human life. You have likely had such experiences too.

Thankfulness is the proper response to the Creator. Every person on earth can do it. Let's start there and see what else He will show us.

[1] *Through Faith Alone,* 365 Devotional Readings from Martin Luther, 1999, Concordia Publishing House, St. Louis.
[2] Arnold Bennett as quoted in *Light From Many Lamps,* edited by Lillian Eichler Watson, Simon and Schuster, New York, 1951, Page 143..

9. Don't discount Christ because of some Christians.

For that matter, don't discount Ghandi because of a handful of strangely robed Hindus. Don't discount California because of certain actors. And so on. We learned long ago the dangers of stereotyping—labeling.

A lawyer friend of mine is suspicious of so-called born again Christians he sees in court. Despite their pious words, they come to court just as greedy as his other clients. "No difference, and sometimes worse," he says.

He shared his latest story as we sat in a sports bar after our weekly racquetball game. A Christian businessman was under contract to buy out his partner who had suddenly developed a career-ending illness. But the Christian guy denied he had a contract and forced the sickly partner to sue him. The sick man could not afford a lengthy court battle, but had no choice.

In court the judgment went against Christian who had broken the contract. Nevertheless, under oath, he said, "Nothing can harm me; I'm under the protective bubble of Jesus." And his pastor was in the courtroom to cheer him on. My lawyer friend called that hypocrisy—and Jesus would have too.

> "The best argument for Christianity is Christians: their joy, their certainty, their completeness. But the strongest argument against Christianity is also Christians—when they are somber, self-righteous, and smug, when they are narrow and repressive, then Christianity dies a thousand deaths."[1]
> —Sheldon Vanauken

Perhaps you've seen the bumper sticker, "Jesus, I believe in you, but protect me from your followers." Bill Maher in his documentary movie, *Religulous,* said to a group of kind-hearted Christian truck drivers who strongly disagreed with him, "Thank you for treating me like Christ [would treat me] and not like Christians."

If you disdain religious hypocrites, you're in good company. Listen to Jesus of Nazareth confronting the Pharisees—learned, highly disciplined teachers of the Jewish law:

> "Woe to you, teachers of the law and Pharisees, you hypocrites! You are like whitewashed tombs, which look beautiful on the outside but on the inside are full of the bones of the dead and everything unclean."
> —Matthew 23:27

Hypocrites don't fool you, and they didn't fool Jesus either. However, now and then, you run into believers who are genuine, likable and don't seem "religious." Study them. Watch how they treat others and what they do when they are alone. Because they are still human, you'll find a few faults, but you'll also find consistency, others-centeredness, joy, and authenticity. Don't throw out the authentic babies with the hypocritical bathwater.

International statesman E. Stanley Jones, a Methodist, told the people of India in the early 1900's: "I will have to apologize for western civilization, for it is only partly Christianized. I will have to apologize for the Christian church, for it, too is only partly Christianized. I will have to apologize for myself again and again, for I'm only a Christian-in-the-making. But when it comes to Jesus Christ, there are no apologies on my lips."[2]

[1] Sheldon Vanauken, *Servant*, September, 1993.

[2] E. Stanley Jones, *Song of Ascents*, Abingdon, Nashville, 1968, page 19.

10. Not all religions lead to God.

On a flight to the East Coast I found myself sitting next to a dark-haired young man who attended prestigious Yale University. Cautiously, I told him I'd never met a Yale student and that he must be pretty smart. He tipped his head to one side, raised one eyebrow and smiled sheepishly. He didn't disagree.

After we were in the air and had settled back in our seats with our Diet Cokes, I said that since Yale began as a school to train preachers, I'd like to ask him a question about God and hear a Yale scholar's response.

"Sure," he said smiling, "But I'm only an undergrad." I liked this kid.

The question: "Do all religions lead to the same God?"

He tipped his head. I flipped over my yellow tablet and quickly drew on the cardboard back a mountain peak with God at the top and three roads at the bottom starting up the mountain at different places. The roads all intersected halfway up but then went in different directions out of sight around the mountain.

"Will they end up in the same place—at God on top of the mountain?" I asked.

He smiled again and furrowed his brow. Did he see what I was asking? Yes. He took a quick sip of his Diet Coke, his eyes never leaving the drawing.

I wondered if he might say that you can't elevate one religion over another. That's called exclusivism—I have the truth and you don't. It's also called intolerance! Or would Yale have taught my new Yale friend the famous quote:

"The proper question to be asked about any creed is not 'Is it pleasant?' but rather, 'Is it true?'"[1]
—Dorothy Sayers

Or perhaps he had heard of a study by Stephen Prothero, chairman of the religion department at nearby Boston University, who summarized: "We are not all on the same one path to the same one God. Religions aren't all saying the same thing. That's presumptuous and wrong. They start with different problems, solve the problems in different ways, and they have different goals.[2]

My Yale friend was squinting his eyes now. I wondered if he had studied anthropology, because surely he would know that many religions, past and present, condone bad stuff. Did Yale teach him that when the kings of some ancient tribes died, a few loyal subjects were thrown in the burial crypt to serve them in the next life and to ward off bad luck for the survivors?[3]

Do all religions lead to God? Does the content of belief matter at all? Or only sincerity?

Now Yale guy was looking at me. He smiled and gave me his answer:

"No," he said, "All religions definitely do not lead to God."

I raised my eyebrows and said, "I'm surprised. Isn't that rather intolerant? Are you saying one belief is better than another?"

"I can't explain it," he said, "but it isn't logical that all beliefs arrive at God—even if the believers are sincere. As the roads on your diagram show, we don't know where they go once they disappear behind the mountain. What basis do we have for saying they reach God at the top?"

He smiled and took another sip of Diet Coke. "Thank you," I said, "You are a credit to Yale even though you are an undergrad."

[1] Dorothy L. Sayers, Worldinvisible.com/library/dlsayers/mindofmaker/mind.01.htm

[2] *USA Today,* March 8, 2007, "Americans get an 'F' in Religion," Cathy Lynn Grossman, page 2D.

[3] *The Great Transformation,* Karen Armstrong, Afred A. Knopf, New York/Toronto, 2006, page 32. Describing the Shang religion of China in 1600 B.C.E., Armstrong describes the ritual sacrifice of a prince's subjects: "As for the men who sacrificed in order to follow him, if he should be a son of heaven, they will be counted in the hundreds or tens."

11. God searches for you more than you search for Him.

Is self-effort the key to finding deeply meaningful spiritual growth? Martin Luther, the famous German reformer of the 1500s, was super-smart and super-disciplined. He climbed the steps of the Holy Vatican in Rome on his knees, confessing his sins over and over, but it did not bring peace with God.

Or, is the search two-way? Maybe God also seeks us? Logically, why would a Creator bring us into existence but then hide from us? Why would the Designer put us in a beautifully designed universe perfectly fitted for life and do nothing more than wish us good luck?

Maybe we should pay more attention to the clues He has left in nature and in the design of the universe. Maybe we should take more seriously a passing word from a friend. And, are some coincidences merely coincidences?

What if we were to assume that God seeks us far more earnestly than we seek him?

Whoso draws nigh to God one step through doubtings dim,
God will advance a mile in blazing light to him.[1]
—Author Unknown

Have you heard the story about Jesus' miraculous healing of a man who had been blind from birth? Suspecting a trick, the religious leaders, the Pharisees, hauled the formerly blind man into an impromptu court and challenged him to admit the healing was a trick. They even questioned his parents as to whether he was truly born blind.

The reply given by the healed man has been made famous by former slave trader, John Newton, in the well-known hymn, "Amazing Grace." The blind man said: "Whether he [Jesus] is a sinner or not, I don't know. One thing I do know. I was blind but now I see!" (John 9:25). But the story doesn't end there. Though the Pharisees found no trickery, they excommunicated him from the temple.

The rest of the story shows Jesus' intentions: "Jesus heard that they had thrown him out, and when he found him, he said, 'Do you believe in the Son of Man?' 'Who is he, sir?' the man asked. 'Tell me so that I may believe in Him.' Jesus said, 'You have now seen him; in fact, he is the one speaking with you,'" (John 9:35-37). The point? Jesus went searching for the blind man and "found him" in his disillusionment.

Similarly, in the classic poem, *The Hound of Heaven,* Francis Thompson (1859-1907) writes:

> I fled Him, down the nights and down the days;
> I fled Him, down the arches of the years;
> I fled Him, down the labyrinthine ways
> Of my own mind; and in the midst of tears
> I hid from Him, and under running laughter.[2]

The poem continues for another 177 lines until Francis Thompson announces that the Hound of Heaven has caught up with him and lovingly touched his life. Was Francis Thompson a learned theologian desperately seeking God? No, he was an opium addict living on the streets.

"If there is a divine being who has created the universe with special concern for us as human beings, then it is entirely reasonable to suppose that, absent our ability to find Him, He would find His way to us."[3]

Does God still "find His way" to people today? Lee Stroebel, award-winning journalist with the *Chicago Tribune,* says yes: "For much of my life I was a skeptic. . . . To me, there was far too much evidence that God was merely a product of wishful thinking, of ancient mythology, of primitive superstition. As far as I was concerned, the case was closed."[4]

But two years later Lee Stroebel surrendered to Christ in a simple prayer. "There were no lightning bolts, no audible replies, no tingly sensations . . . there was something else that was equally exhilarating: there was the rush of reason."[5]

Was Lee Stroebel seeking God? Not outwardly. But I have yet to meet a person who is not in someway searching for satisfaction, truth and joy.

Is God trying to find you? Assuredly yes! But rather than running (like Francis Thompson) let Him find you by responding to the clues . . . a word of truth from a kindly friend . . . a memory . . . a coincidence . . . beautiful artwork . . . a gorgeous sunrise . . . a Bible verse mysteriously popping into your mind. And say "thank you" for the wonderful creation of which you are a part!

He is lovingly searching for you. Stop running. Surrender. Tell Him you are ready for the next step.

"Can one reach God by toil? He gives himself to the pure in heart.
He asks nothing but our attention."[6]
—W. B. Yeats, Irish poet and mystic

[1] *Pathways To Spiritual Power,* Compiled by Thomas S. Kepler, The World Publishing Company, Cleveland, 1952, page 101.

[2] *The Oxford Book of English Mystical Verse,* Nicholson and Lee, eds. 1917. Bartleby.com (Great Books Online)

[3] Dinesh D'Souza, *What's So Great About Christianity?* Tyndale, Carol Stream, IL, 2007, page 201.

[4] *The Case for Christ,* Lee Stroebel; Zondervan, Grand Rapids, 1998, page 13.

[5] Ibid, page 269.

[6] *The Daily Bible Study Series (Volume 2),* The Gospel of Matthew, William Barclay, The Westminster Press, Philadelphia, 1975, page 16.

12. Jesus is different.

On the first day of my Western Civilization class at college the professor said, "There is no evidence for Jesus outside the New Testament." Five hundred nervous, hoping-for-A's-freshmen faithfully wrote it down as truth. But I found out later it isn't true. Scholars today find many historical evidences for the life of Jesus outside the Bible. In fact, compared with other ancient religious leaders, the evidence for Jesus is far more historically reliable.[1]

I mentioned earlier that Jesus of Nazareth attracts me more than other religious leaders. Something about him is different. It is true that Jesus, Buddha, Mohammed, Confucious, and even Hollywood spiritualists all teach some form of the Golden Rule—to "do unto others as you would have them do unto you." But a simple review of Jesus' life shows him to be unique in three major ways:

1. Jesus claimed to be God. Not *a* god, not *like* a god, not a prophet representing God. He claimed to be the transcendent monotheistic God of the Jewish people— the Uncaused Cause. Other leaders point to God (or gods) but none claim to actually *be* God.

Unfortunately, through the centuries Jesus has been "reimagined." Some say he is only a:

- great teacher;
- misunderstood prophet who accidentally got into trouble;
- revolutionary who sought to change the system—but still only a human.

The 1970's hippie Broadway musical *Jesus Christ Superstar* says he's "just a man." Maybe an unusual man, but still just a man.

A few years ago a friend told me Jesus himself never claimed to be God, but that his followers added that moniker years later to invent Christianity. This is also the message of the *Davinci Code* book and movie. I said, "What if I could show you that Jesus *himself* claimed to be God?" He replied, "That would be scary!"

Yes, it is scary, because that would change everything! Here's an incident in Jesus' life that contradicts the *Davinci Code:*

Jesus' practice of forgiving sins angered the Jewish leaders. "Who can forgive sins but God alone?" they accurately reasoned. Finally they'd had enough and picked up stones to stone him—not to scare him, but to kill him. Jesus asked for which of his good works they were stoning him. "We are not stoning you for any of these," replied the Jews, "but for blasphemy, because you, a mere man, claim to be God" (John 10:33).

There it is—his claim to divinity spoken not from his own lips or by his followers, but by his enemies. Make no mistake—Jesus claimed to be divine! Scary!

2. Jesus claimed to forgive sins. If I say something unkind to you, you can choose to forgive me for that one transgression. But you are not in a position to forgive me for *all* my transgressions. Only a lunatic or a transcendent Being would claim to do that.

Jesus intended for the world to know he had the ability to grant forgiveness. The evening before he died he hosted a "last supper" with his mentorees where he passed around the traditional Jewish cup of wine. But this time was different.

> *Then he took the cup, gave thanks and offered it to them, saying,*
> *"Drink from it all of you.*
> *This is my blood of the covenant, which is poured out for **many***
> *for the forgiveness of sins."*
> —Matthew 26:27-28

Note that he offered forgiveness of sins for "many," not for his followers only.
Perhaps you've seen the bumper sticker: Christians aren't perfect—just forgiven.
Okay, I wish they were better drivers. Nonetheless, is there a truth here?
Sin? That's the stuff that other people do—like throwing a cigarette butt out a car
window. Or abusing a child. Or big-industry polluting a stream.
Big or little, acknowledging sin implies we are guilty of something—and that is a
conversation stopper. Garrison Keilor of the radio show, *A Prairie Home Companion*,
jokes about his church—Our Lady of Perpetual Guilt. But don't we all live with a
good dose of "would-of, could-of, should-of?"

Let's admit it, sin is hard to talk about—especially if it is connected to me! I'm not a criminal! New York author Tim Keller in *The Reason for God* says sin is: "Putting good things in the place of God." We're all guilty!

Is today's preoccupation on personal maximization—putting "good things in the place of God"—just a bandaid over a cancer? What about the father who divorces his wife because raising their baby girl cuts into his free time? Self-centeredness is another simple definition of sin.

> *Who can say, "I have kept my heart pure; I am clean and without sin"?*
> *—Proverbs 20:9*

Could we not experience more freedom, peace, and joy by humbly confessing our sins to a loving Someone who has earned the right to say, "You are forgiven?"

3. Jesus resurrected—He came back to life from the dead. Siddhartha Gautama (Buddha) died at age 80 lying on his side in a meditative trance between two trees after experiencing food poisoning.[2] Muhammed, the prophet of Islam, died June 8, 632 B.C., after a long illness.[3] By contrast, Jesus didn't die of old age or illness. He was killed by crucifixion, the most cruel form of death in the ancient world. And the historical documents say he miraculously came back to life after three days in the tomb.

Some skeptics say a "substitute" Jesus resurrected. Jesus escaped from the Roman guards into the mob at the crucifixion site, and they crucified the wrong guy. Others say Jesus didn't die on the cross but merely swooned and regained consciousness in the coolness of the rock tomb—like the South African who woke up in the coolness of the morgue after his family determined he was dead![4]

But the popular "swoon theory" is disproven by the crucifixion story itself. After Jesus had hung on the cross for six hours a Roman soldier speared him in the side. The text says "blood and water" came out. We know today that crucifixion victims suffered hypovolemic shock which causes fluid to gather in the sack around the heart and lungs. The spear in Jesus' side probably pierced both heart and lungs resulting in an issue of pleural effusion (water) as well as blood.[5] Jesus was dead.

Scholars such as Lew Wallace, author of the classic, *Ben Hur*, studied the resurrection objectively hoping to disprove it. But instead they found compelling evidence that the laws of physics were broken early one morning in the spring of 34 A.D. by the One who created the laws of physics, in order to communicate love to you and me. The resurrection really happened. Even sources outside the New Testament refer to Jesus as a historical figure and that he was crucified and that his followers claimed he was alive.

Since that first day of the week when Jesus was found to be alive, followers of Christ greet one another on Easter morning with the phrase, "He is risen."

To summarize, three major facts regarding the resurrection cannot be ignored:

a. The empty tomb. The Romans or Jewish leaders could have debunked the resurrection simply by producing the dead corpse of Jesus from the tomb. But they could not. Matthew 28:11-15 says the authorities bribed the guards to spread the story that the disciples had stolen the body while the guards were sleeping—the same fearful disciples who fled when Jesus was arrested.

b. Many eyewitnesses, including women. Women were the first eyewitnesses to see Jesus alive. But women were of such low social status that their testimony was not even admissible in court. Poor choices for eyewitnesses—unless it really happened!

c. Martyrdom of the witnesses. History shows that Jesus' original disciples were martyred for their trust in him—they would not recant their belief in his resurrection even under threat of death. Men and women will die for deeply held beliefs, but they will not die for something they know to be a hoax.

Okay, what if Jesus *is* unique? Only this: If he is who he said he was, then he must be taken seriously. Casually brushing him aside as a Wizard of Oz or a good moral teacher denies the evidence of history. British historian C.S. Lewis famously said that viewing Jesus as merely a good moral teacher "is not an option He has left open to us."

Instead, consider this: Sacrificial genuine love cannot be ignored. It creates in us a

desire to respond. "Love is most persuasive when it involves sacrifice."[6]
Jesus has done something quite nice for us. His death on the cross gave him authority to forgive our sins. We no longer need to figure out ways to relieve true guilt, false guilt, childhood woundings, and dysfunctional baggage. In other worldviews, people die or are killed for their gods, but only in Jesus has God died for his people.

[1] *The Case for Christ*, Lee Stroebel, Zondervan, Grand Rapids, 1998, pages 79,86. A famous example is a quote from the Jewish historian Josephus who wrote near the end of the first century. "About this time there lived Jesus, a wise man, if indeed one might call him a man. For he was one who wrought surprising feats and was a teacher of such people as accept the truth gladly. He won over many Jews and many of the Greeks. He was the Christ. When Pilate, upon hearing him accused by men of the highest standing among us, had condemned him to be crucified, those who had in the first place come to love him did not give up their affection for him. On the third day he appeared to them restored to life, for the prophets of God had prophesied these and countless other marvelous things about him. And the tribe of Christians, so called after him, has still to this day not disappeared."

[2] Ibid, page 101.

[3] *Worldviews*, John Yeats and John Blasé, Think, Colorado Springs, CO, 2006, page 83.

[4] *The Gazette*, July 26, 2011, Associated Press, by Nastasya Tay, Johannesburg, page 1.

[5] www.gotquestions.org/blood-water-Jesus.html Many writers have addressed this question of the blood and water with nearly identical answers.

[6] Disappointment with God, Philip Yancey, Zondervan, Grand Rapids, 1988, page 122.

13. What's next?

I can't tell you. This is your journey. But I can say confidently that a loving Creator is seeking you. From my own experience, I know that continuing in a moral drift scenario is dangerous. I can also tell you that going-it-alone is not wise. The Creator brings others around you to assist you in your journey, and maybe for you to assist them.

Because you are a learner—or want to be, maybe offer this prayer:

"Spirit of truth . . .

"If you are out there I'd like to find you—actually I'd like you to find me! I'd like to experience you in truthful, authentic ways. But I fear it won't work.

"I don't want to be like some ugly-acting, hypocritical people I know, but I don't want to miss you because I'm skeptical of them.

"But I know enough to say, 'Thank you for creating me.' And I am committed to discovering truth. I'm starting there.

"Also, I admit something is not right with me. I have this self-loathing malaise. I admit I am self-centered. And I know that just trying harder won't help.

"If you are there, please find me. Maybe send someone to tell me about you. Or send me a dream or a coincidence or a memory from my past. I'll watch for clues.

"Okay…."

What's next?

We want to hear from you. Please let us know what you thought of this booklet and how we might encourage you further in your spiritual life. Contact us at www.navpress.com. Thank you.

Dawson**Media**

To order additional copies visit NavPress.com